Animal Groups

Worms

By Dalton Rains

www.littlebluehousebooks.com

Copyright © 2024 by Little Blue House, Mendota Heights, MN 55120. All rights reserved. No part of this book may be reproduced or utilized in any form or by any means without written permission from the publisher.

Little Blue House is distributed by North Star Editions:
sales@northstareditions.com | 888-417-0195

Produced for Little Blue House by Red Line Editorial.

Photographs ©: Shutterstock Images, cover, 7, 9, 11, 12–13, 15, 17, 21, 22–23, 24 (top left), 24 (top right), 24 (bottom left), 24 (bottom right); iStockphoto, 4, 19

Library of Congress Control Number: 2023902026

ISBN
978-1-64619-813-9 (hardcover)
978-1-64619-842-9 (paperback)
978-1-64619-899-3 (ebook pdf)
978-1-64619-871-9 (hosted ebook)

Printed in the United States of America
Mankato, MN
082023

About the Author

Dalton Rains writes and edits nonfiction children's books. He lives in Minnesota.

Table of Contents

Worms **5**

Is It a Worm? **22**

Glossary **24**

Index **24**

Worms

I see a worm.

It has a long body.

I see a worm.

It has many parts.

I see many worms.

They live in soil.

I see a worm.

It lives in water.

I see a worm.

It eats other animals.

I see a worm.

It has a flat body.

I see a worm.

It has colors and spots.

I see a worm.

It has a round body.

I see a worm.

It is very small.

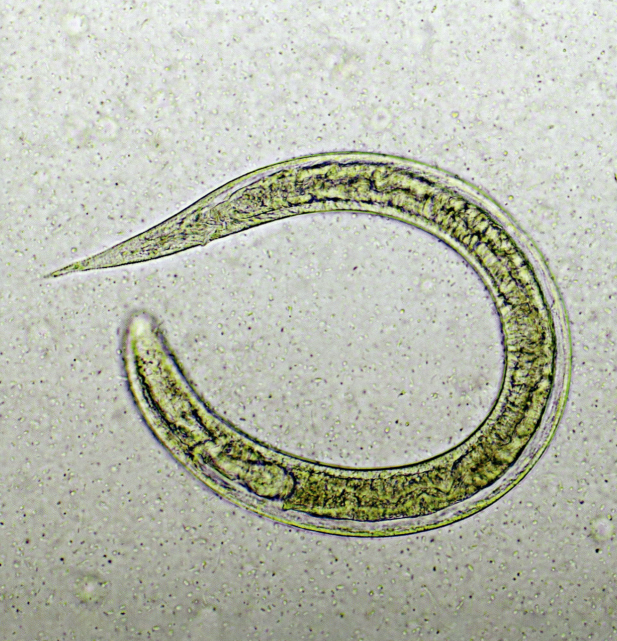

Is It a Worm?

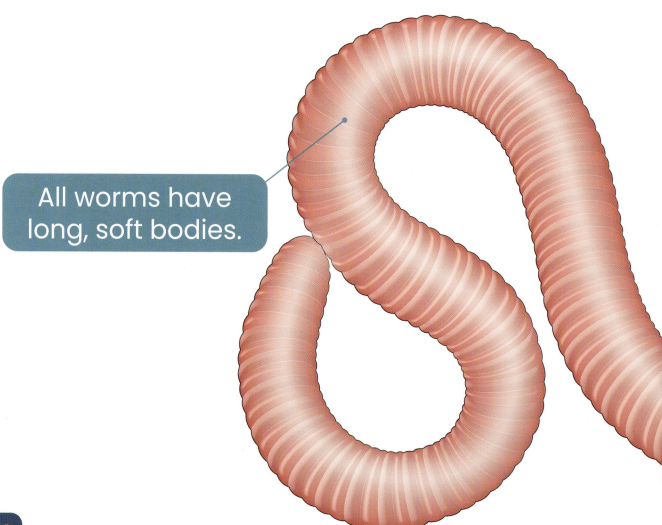

All worms have long, soft bodies.

22

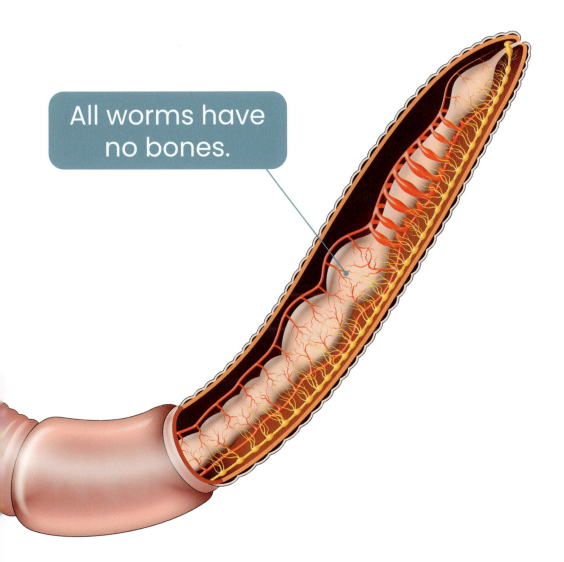

Glossary

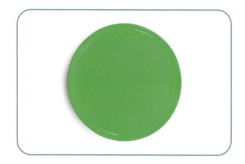
round

spots

soil

water

Index

A
animals, 12

C
colors, 16

F
flat, 14

S
small, 20